GW01458797

The Who What Where Quiz Book

By Kate & Steve Haywood

Thanks to Toby, Dylan & family for inspiring us to write this book and your awesome help testing it for us!

Copyright © 2022 Kate & Steve Haywood

All rights reserved.

Introduction

Welcome to The Ultimate Who, What, Where Quiz Book. This is a little different to our regular quiz books. It has come about due to feedback from our previous books – lots of different people liked these types of quizzes so we thought we would make a book just about them.

First of all, each page is one single quiz with one answer. Your aim is to follow the twelve clues and see how quickly you can identify the person or character, place or thing. Can you do it in six or eight, or for some do you need all twelve clues? If playing with family and friends and want to make it more challenging, give them a limit of perhaps 3 or 5 guesses per round!

Also, for this quiz book you will find the answers at the back. This is a change from our usual format, and has allowed us to put lots of extra quizzes in the book by not having the answer directly on the next page. We have randomised the answers, so it is more difficult to accidentally see the answer to the next quiz.

We hope you enjoy this quiz book. If you like it, please consider writing a review, it will really help more people to find and enjoy our books. We've also written other quiz books for your enjoyment (or they make good gifts!), just search for us on Amazon. Thank you!

Also, if you like the books, do look at the other books we've got available. Visit our website at quiziclebooks.com for more details and to sign up for our newsletter – plus we're offering a **completely FREE subscriber only quiz book** when you sign up. There's also our Facebook page which is a great place to keep up with what we've got going on – just head on over to facebook.com/quiziclebooks.

Happy Quizzing!

Kate & Steve

Quiz 1

You are looking for – a thing

1. I am colourful
2. The first known physical appearance of me in any form, is from 470 million years ago
3. I appear in songs by Billy Joel and The Rolling Stones
4. My safety is so important
5. I can be used in warfare
6. You can control me
7. I appear in book titles by Stephen King and Celeste Ng
8. I am a chemical process
9. You can insure against me
10. I am a type of Amazon Kindle
11. I am hot
12. I cook and burn

The answer for this quiz is number 12.

All answers are at the back of the book.

Quiz 2

You are looking for – a place

1. I am a city
2. My flag is red and black with white crosses
3. My country's National Opera and Ballet is housed in the Stopera here
4. The Christmas tree for my famous square is traditionally grown in the German Ardennes
5. A coffee is called koffie here
6. Cycling is a very popular method of travel in this city
7. One of my biggest parks is called the Vondelpark
8. My nearest airport is called Schiphol
9. You can find well-known art here in the Rijksmuseum
10. I have a large canal network
11. You can visit the Anne Frank House here
12. I am the capital of The Netherlands

The answer for this quiz is number 50.

All answers are at the back of the book.

Quiz 3

You are looking for – a person or character

1. I am male
2. I have a red house
3. My eyes have been described as green, but they appear to be blue
4. My father is dead
5. I am a character
6. I share a birthday with my creator
7. My first book had a print run of 1,000 copies
8. My creator was approached by Michael Jackson to collaborate on a musical about me, but she refused
9. My books were the first children's books to make the New York Times Bestseller List since *Charlotte's Web* in 1952
10. I go to a famous school
11. I travel from King's Cross station
12. I am a wizard

The answer for this quiz is number 72.

All answers are at the back of the book.

Quiz 4

You are looking for - a year

1. Online dating site eHarmony was launched
2. The last ever *Peanuts* comic was printed
3. The film *Miss Congeniality* was released
4. Bill Gates stepped down as CEO of Microsoft
5. The *Malcolm in the Middle* TV show began
6. Alec Guinness died
7. Pete Sampras won the Wimbledon tennis tournament
8. Nancy Pelosi became the first female Speaker of the House in the USA
9. Britney Spears released *Oops I Did It Again*
10. The population of the world was 6,037,653,405 on 1st January of this year
11. George W Bush was elected 43rd President of the USA
12. I am considered to be the millennium

The answer for this quiz is number 27.

All answers are at the back of the book.

Quiz 5

You are looking for – a person or character

1. I am a real person
2. I am male
3. I taught for around 45 years
4. I died of Pig-bel disease which is a fatal type of food poisoning
5. I am religious
6. My birth was in 563 BCE or 480 BCE according to tradition
7. I am well known for meditation and mind training
8. My real name was *Siddhārtha Gautama*
9. I was cremated
10. My name means 'awakened one' or 'enlightened one'
11. My teaching is based on ending with a state of Nirvana
12. I created Buddhism

The answer for this quiz is number 39.

All answers are at the back of the book.

Quiz 6

You are looking for – a thing

1. My name is Latin
2. I am marked
3. I am circular
4. I have a link to Cancer
5. I am part of nature
6. I can be celestial
7. I am linked to three oceans
8. I am the centre of a circle
9. You can find me halfway
10. I am over 25,000 miles or 40,000 km long
11. I go through 11 countries
12. I divide the Earth

The answer for this quiz is number 2.

All answers are at the back of the book.

Quiz 7

You are looking for – a thing

1. I was discovered in 600BC
2. I am essential to modern life
3. Some think that the Egyptians may have used me
4. English Physician William Gilbert first used my Latin name
5. I give my name to a sea creature
6. I can be a natural phenomenon
7. I am current
8. I am linked to Benjamin Franklin
9. You can do a circuit with me
10. I have many, many uses
11. I am linked to Michael Faraday
12. I travel at the speed of light

The answer for this quiz is number 63.

All answers are at the back of the book.

Quiz 8

You are looking for – a thing

1. For some, I am fun
2. You can find me in the home
3. I am the result of various forces
4. I cannot exist in space
5. I am partially liquid
6. I freeze at 0 °C or 32F
7. Light can reflect on my surface
8. You can make me with a wand
9. I may be partially formed of soap
10. I am hollow
11. I am in some drinks
12. I am often found in baths

The answer for this quiz is number 20.

All answers are at the back of the book.

Quiz 9

You are looking for – a person or character

1. I am male
2. I am known to be extremely clever
3. I am on the television and in films
4. I am also known for being eccentric
5. I was mentioned in The Strand magazine in 1891
6. There is a British 50p piece linked to me
7. I am a character
8. I play the violin
9. I am a detective
10. My story is written by Sir Arthur Conan Doyle
11. My partner is called Dr Watson
12. I live at 221B Baker Street

The answer for this quiz is number 75.

All answers are at the back of the book.

Quiz 10

You are looking for – a year

1. Frank Hornby of Liverpool is granted a patent for the toy that would become Meccano
2. New York becomes the first US State to require vehicle numbers or license plates
3. The first UK Fingerprint Bureau is established at Scotland Yard in London
4. Emily Hobhouse reports cruel conditions in the Second Boer War concentration camps
5. *The Tale of Peter Rabbit* by Beatrix Potter is released
6. Hubert Cecil Booth patents an electric vacuum cleaner in the UK
7. U.S. Steel is incorporated by J.P.Morgan
8. Louis Armstrong is born in this year
9. A showing of 71 Vincent Van Gogh paintings in Paris becomes a sensation, 10 years after he died
10. The first Nobel Prize ceremony took place
11. William McKinley, US President is assassinated
12. Queen Victoria of the UK died

The answer for this quiz is number 32.

All answers are at the back of the book.

Quiz 11

You are looking for - a place

1. I am home to both desert and rainforest
2. Islam is my biggest religion
3. In a sense, everyone comes from me
4. Many of my children were stolen from me
5. My people speak about 2000 different languages
6. The longest river in the world starts and ends in me
7. Lots of countries have fought over me
8. I am home to the world's fastest and biggest animals
9. I am home to the world's largest desert
10. I am the title of a song by Toto
11. I am a continent
12. Some of my most popular tourist attractions include Table Mountain, Serengeti National Park and the Great Pyramids

The answer for this quiz is number 53.

All answers are at the back of the book.

Quiz 12

You are looking for – a person or character

1. I am female
2. I am a character
3. My first author was Robert Southey
4. In my original story I was an old woman
5. My story involves animals
6. My story has been made into films and the first one was in 1934
7. I am a well-known children's story
8. These days in my story, I am a young girl
9. I am hungry in my story
10. I am sleepy in my story
11. I have blonde hair
12. I upset three bears in my story

The answer for this quiz is number 4.

All answers are at the back of the book.

Quiz Number 13

You are looking for – a thing

1. Children love me
2. My album was extremely popular
3. I am based on a story by Hans Christian Anderson
4. I am a film
5. The concept of the film first began at the studios that made me, in 1940
6. One of my main characters was meant to be evil, but ended up being good
7. I involve siblings
8. I won two Academy Awards
9. I was released in 2013
10. I took 1.28 billion dollars at the box office
11. I am a Disney film
12. I am set in Arendelle
13. One of my characters is a talking snowman

The answer for this quiz is number 41.

All answers are at the back of the book.

Quiz 14

You are looking for – a place

1. My religion is predominantly Christian
2. My population is around 28 million
3. My flag is white, red and green
4. Humans have destroyed more than, 90% of my natural forests in the last 2,350 years
5. I have two official languages, one only really spoken here and the other is French
6. My capital is Antananarivo
7. I was once a French colony
8. I lie in the Indian Ocean
9. There is a well-known 2005 animated film about me
10. I am an island country
11. Most of my species are found nowhere else in the world
12. Lemurs are found here in the wild, the only place on Earth

The answer for this quiz is number 13.

All answers are at the back of the book.

Quiz 15

You are looking for – a thing

1. I am an instrument
2. I am an everyday item
3. People always want me to give them more
4. A mechanical version of me was created in Europe in 1300
5. An electric version of me was patented in 1840
6. I can go on strike
7. Early versions of me used water
8. I feature numbers or symbols
9. I typically use a harmonic oscillator
10. I am split into twelve segments
11. I have hands
12. You might hear me tick

The answer for this quiz is number 65.

All answers are at the back of the book.

Quiz 16

You are looking for – a person or character

1. I am male
2. I live my life in the public eye
3. I hold citizenship of three countries including Canada
4. I have a bachelor's degree from the University of Pennsylvania
5. I have been sued several times
6. I was born in 1971
7. I have a brother called Kimbal and a sister called Tosca
8. I co-founded PayPal
9. I have made many cameos in films and TV series including *Iron Man 2* and *The Big Bang Theory*
10. I am South African
11. I am an entrepreneur
12. I founded SpaceX in 2002

The answer for this quiz is number 22.

All answers are at the back of the book.

Quiz 17

You are looking for – a thing

1. I involve a lot of people
2. Most of the people have one or more skills
3. A part of me is hot
4. I am known to cost a lot of money
5. Often North Korea is involved with me
6. Pierre de Coubertin founded me
7. I am an event
8. I am Greek in origin
9. I began in 1896
10. I involve people from most countries
11. I feature five rings
12. I am usually held every four years

The answer for this quiz is number 31.

All answers are at the back of the book.

Quiz 18

You are looking for – a place

1. I am roughly circular
2. I am very large
3. I am very cold
4. When I am drawn, I am typically yellow or orange
5. There are many images of me these days
6. Ancient Babylonians first found me
7. I am far away
8. There is ice and rock inside me
9. I have a red spot
10. I am named after a Roman god
11. I have a moon called Ganymede
12. I am a planet

The answer for this quiz is number 74.

All answers are at the back of the book.

Quiz 19

You are looking for – a person or character

1. I have seen many, many birthdays
2. I was born in London
3. I was on the cover of *Time* magazine as a child
4. I have travelled far and wide
5. I am female
6. My mother was also famous and died in 2002
7. I married for love
8. I never speak much about politics
9. I am a Christian
10. I have loved horses all my life
11. I have seen many jubilees
12. I am a Queen

The answer for this quiz is number 51.

All answers are at the back of the book.

Quiz 20

You are looking for – a place

1. I am coastal
2. History suggests I was once part of something bigger
3. I am mild in the winter and warm in the summer
4. I touch Italy
5. Historically nations have sought to dominate me
6. I am nearly landlocked, if you think about it
7. In Roman times I was called Mare Nostrum
8. I have stable biodiversity
9. I lead to many spelling mistakes
10. I am a body of water
11. I have a coastline of around 46,000km
12. I surround many islands

The answer for this quiz is number 5.

All answers are at the back of the book.

Quiz 21

You are looking for – a thing

1. I am 79
2. Hieroglyphics from 2,600 BC describe me
3. I used to be of a set standard
4. I can be dissolved in cyanide and mercury
5. As of 2020 over 200,000 tonnes of me exists above ground
6. When I am pure, I am soft and malleable
7. It is worth investing in me
8. My chemical symbol is Au
9. I can be panned for
10. I am spoken about in carats
11. Finish this phrase from Shakespeare's *The Merchant of Venice*, "All that glitters is not ____"
12. I am the main constituent of traditional wedding rings

The answer for this quiz is number 42.

All answers are at the back of the book.

Quiz 22

You are looking for – a person or character

1. I have only been famous for a short time
2. I am outspoken
3. I have received many honours and awards including the Keys to the City of Montreal
4. I have met Pope Francis
5. At least 5 newly discovered species have been named after me including a new species of beetle from Kenya in 2019
6. One of my middle names is Tintin
7. I have Asperger's Syndrome
8. I wrote a book called *No One Is Too Small to Make a Difference*
9. I am a young woman
10. I support truancy for important issues
11. I am Swedish
12. I am a climate activist

The answer for this quiz is number 60.

All answers are at the back of the book.

Quiz Number 23

You are looking for – a thing

1. I started in the US
2. I began in 1994
3. I moved internationally in 1998
4. I have struck up agreements with others over the years, but they were not all successful
5. I have a lot of subsidiaries including Goodreads and Twitch
6. There are over 20 websites that are a direct part of me
7. I am one of the biggest companies in the world
8. I have well over a million employees
9. I was founded by Jeff Bezos
10. I am known for Alexa
11. My logo is fashioned around A to Z with an arrow
12. I have been criticised recently over counterfeiting, poor working conditions and tax avoidance

The answer for this quiz is number 14.

All answers are at the back of the book.

Quiz 24

You are looking for – a thing

1. I involve water
2. I can float
3. I date from 1911
4. There was a lot of excitement surrounding me
5. Millvina Dean is an important name associated with me
6. I was 269 metres long
7. I am now a cautionary tale
8. Edward J. Smith was in charge of me
9. My sisters were Olympic and Britannic
10. A very famous film was made about me with Kate Winslet and Leonardo DiCaprio
11. I collided with an iceberg
12. Over 1,500 people died when I sank including John Jacob Astor IV, one of the richest people in the world

The answer for this quiz is number 25.

All answers are at the back of the book.

Quiz 25

You are looking for – a person or character

1. I am an actor
2. I was born in Washington D.C.
3. My first film was *Ragtime* in 1981
4. I have around 200 credits as an actor
5. I was born in 1948
6. I had a minor role in *Coming to America* but wasn't well-known at the time
7. My middle name is Leroy
8. As a child I went to segregated schools
9. In the 1980s I worked for three years as a stand-in for Bill Cosby on *The Cosby Show*
10. I am the highest grossing actor of all time – films I have appeared in have grossed over $27 billion.
11. I play Mace Windu in the Star Wars series of films
12. I play Nick Fury in the Marvel series of films
13. My most famous stand-alone film is probably *Pulp Fiction*

The answer for this quiz is number 70.

All answers are at the back of the book.

Quiz 26

You are looking for – a thing

1. I was published in 1935
2. I am colourful
3. I am not suitable for small children
4. I involve economic principles
5. I have a large number of spin-offs, but none are as successful as my original version
6. Rumours of a film have been circulating since 2008, but there is already a documentary about me
7. I was inspired by the 1903 Landlord's Game by Lizzie Magie
8. Since 2017 I have included a penguin, a tyrannosaurus and a rubber duck
9. My current company reports that the longest ever play of me took 70 days
10. I involve a pair of dice
11. If you want to play, you will need my money
12. I am all about buying properties

The answer for this quiz is number 33.

All answers are at the back of the book.

Quiz 27

You are looking for – a place

1. I have a subtropical hot desert climate
2. Around 40% of my grass content was banned due to drought and to conserve water
3. I am known for entertainment
4. I am a city
5. You can visit The Mob Museum downtown
6. My name means "The Meadows" in Spanish
7. I am in the USA
8. Red Rock Canyon National Conservation area is nearby
9. My dancing fountains are so popular, The Fountains of Bellagio
10. I am in Nevada
11. In the film *Ocean's 11*, the heists take place here
12. You can play the slots or high roller poker here

The answer for this quiz is number 52.

All answers are at the back of the book.

Quiz 28

You are looking for – a thing

1. I am entertaining
2. I am American
3. I involve something historical
4. I also involve a type of science
5. I am mostly in Central America
6. I am a film
7. My director was born in 1946
8. Two of my main characters are Ellie and Alan
9. I began in 1993 with a budget of $63 million
10. I am set on a fictional island called Isla Nublar
11. I feature several sequels with actor Chris Pratt
12. I involve a T-Rex and velociraptors

The answer for this quiz is number 6.

All answers are at the back of the book.

Quiz 29

You are looking for – a person or character

1. I am a woman
2. My known name is one of my middle names and my first name is really Magdalena
3. When I was young, I had Polio
4. I was disabled by a bus accident at 18 years old
5. I am from Mexico
6. I am an artist known for my strong facial features
7. I draw inspiration from folk culture and my paintings tend to be colourful
8. Actor Edward G Robinson purchased 4 of my paintings for $800 in 1938
9. I am part of the Surrealist and Magic Surrealism Movements
10. I died in 1954 aged 47
11. My home La Casa Azul is now a museum dedicated to me
12. Some of my famous paintings are Broken Column, The Wounded Deer and Without Hope

The answer for this quiz is number 44.

All answers are at the back of the book.

Quiz 30

You are looking for – a thing

1. I am inscribed
2. I attract over a million visitors each year
3. My creation involved 22,000 people
4. I am on the bank of the river Yamuna
5. I am a landmark
6. I was built by a man commemorating his wife
7. Elephants were involved in my construction
8. I am a building
9. I involve many architectural styles
10. I have domes
11. I am in India
12. I am made from white marble

The answer for this quiz is number 61.

All answers are at the back of the book.

Quiz 31

You are looking for – a year

1. A severe frost in England freezes the river Thames
2. The first merry-go-round is seen at a fair, in Turkey
3. Shōgun Tokugawa Hidetada restores Osaka Castle
4. The Battle of White Mountain occurs during the Thirty Years War
5. Thomas Campion the English poet and composer dies – he wrote over 100 lute songs and masques
6. James I of England sits on the throne at this time
7. The Wampanoag tribe of native Americans meet white Europeans for the first time
8. 13 days of snow blankets Scotland and of a flock of 20,000 sheep on Eskdale Moor only 35 survive
9. Peregrine White is born
10. Diego Velázquez finishes the painting The Nun Jerónima de la Fuente
11. The mother of astronomer and mathematician Johannes Kepler is arrested for witchcraft
12. The Mayflower arrives in New England, USA

The answer for this quiz is number 15.

All answers are at the back of the book.

Quiz 32

You are looking for – a person or a character

1. I am male
2. I have been played by multiple actors
3. Several people have written about me including Sebastian Faulks and Anthony Horowitz
4. My 'nephew' had a TV series from 1991-1992
5. There are lots of people out to get me
6. I love my gadgets
7. Two of the actors that played me have been knighted
8. My story was originally penned by Ian Fleming who wrote *Chitty, Chitty, Bang, Bang*
9. Two of my theme songs were sung by A-ha and Matt Monro
10. Two of my films are *For Your Eyes Only* and *You Only Live Twice*
11. You know me as 007
12. I like my martinis shaken not stirred

The answer for this quiz is number 23.

All answers are at the back of the book.

Quiz 33

You are looking for – a thing

1. I am an animal
2. I can be male or female
3. I can be found in almost every part of the world
4. There are over 3,000 species of me
5. I can be royal
6. Different breeds of me can survive in different places including forests and deserts
7. I can travel up to 12 miles an hour
8. I can pose a risk to humans
9. I have a bad reputation going back many years
10. I smell with my tongue
11. I can be venomous
12. Two famous characters of me are Jafar and Nagini

The answer for this quiz is number 35.

All answers are at the back of the book.

Quiz 34

You are looking for – a thing

1. I am the most popular of my kind
2. I can only be used on certain days
3. Women buy more of me than men
4. I am typically sentimental
5. I can be funny or serious
6. I can be any size, although I am unlikely to be very large
7. I can be matt or glossy
8. I grow on trees
9. Evidence has been found of a type of me on a wooden tablet dating from the Roman period
10. In my current form I appeared in mid-19th century Britain
11. Most people celebrate with me
12. I wish you greetings on the anniversary of your birth

The answer for this quiz is number 69.

All answers are at the back of the book

Quiz 35

You are looking for – a person or character

1. I am female
2. I like children
3. I enjoy singing
4. You can see me on the stage and in film
5. At one point, Angela Lansbury and Bette Davis were considered to play me
6. I have an umbrella
7. In the film *Saving Mr. Banks*, the main character's daughters beg him to make a film about me
8. The main character is Walt Disney, and he did end up making the film eventually
9. My first film gained 13 Academy Award nominations, the most for a Disney film at the time
10. My books were written by P.L. Travers
11. I was played by Julie Andrews and Emily Blunt
12. I often say that a spoonful of sugar helps the medicine go down

The answer for this quiz is number 49.

All answers are at the back of the book.

Quiz 36

You are looking for – a place

1. I am 42,800 square miles and bigger than some people think
2. I am a country
3. For some time, I was a colony of Spain and one of my main languages is a Spanish variant
4. The project "La alegria de vivir" makes my city colourful
5. I am an island
6. Tobacco and sugar are two of my big exports
7. Classic cars are popular on my streets
8. Winston Churchill was a big fan of my cigars Romeo y Julieta
9. My exports are still banned in the USA
10. Che Guevara was a major figure in a revolution here
11. Fidel Castro was the leader here for almost 50 years
12. My capital is Havana

The answer for this quiz is number 8.

All answers are at the back of the book.

Quiz 37

You are looking for – a thing

1. I can come in many colours
2. You might be able to smell me
3. You can find me both outside and inside
4. My oldest remains are from the late Eocene Florissant Formation of Colorado (fossil beds)
5. Today's version of me comes from 18th century China
6. Some varieties of me are named after famous people such as Charles Darwin and Roald Dahl
7. I might be tea, dog or damask
8. I am a plant
9. I can be a person's name
10. I am a flower
11. I often flavour Turkish delight
12. My red version is considered to be the most romantic flower

The answer for this quiz is number 57.

All answers are at the back of the book.

Quiz 38

You are looking for – a person/ character

1. I have a very famous family name
2. I am a Roman Catholic
3. I published a book that won the Pulitzer Prize
4. I went to Harvard University
5. I am buried in Arlington National Cemetery
6. I had a son named after me who died in a plane crash
7. I was in the United States Naval Reserve during the Second World War
8. I was a political figure during the Cold War
9. I was born at 83 Beals Street in Boston
10. I married socialite Jacqueline Onassis
11. I was an American President
12. I was assassinated in 1963

The answer for this quiz is number 29.

All answers are at the back of the book.

Quiz 39

You are looking for – a place

1. I used to be known to Europeans as Marañón
2. I used to go in the opposite direction
3. I am South American
4. I come from the Mantaro River
5. You can find me in three countries
6. I am in Brazil
7. I end at the Atlantic Ocean
8. I am surrounded by a lot of rainforest
9. My mouth is bigger than some countries
10. I am a body of water
11. I am almost 7,000 km long
12. For a long time people thought I was the longest river in the world although that is disputed

The answer for this quiz is number 45.

All answers are at the back of the book.

Quiz 40

You are looking for – a person or character

1. I have a star on the Hollywood Walk of Fame
2. I am involved with films
3. I have won three Academy Awards
4. In 2013 *Time* magazine listed me as one of the 100 Most Important People of the Century
5. I am male
6. One of my first films was *The Sugarland Express*
7. In 1996, *Life* magazine named me as the most influential person of my generation
8. My net worth was estimated by Forbes magazine as $3.7 billion in 2020
9. I was born in 1946
10. I am a director
11. Seven of my films have been inducted into the National Film Registry by the Library of Congress for being culturally, historically or aesthetically significant
12. I directed *Jaws* and *Saving Private Ryan*

The answer for this quiz is number 34.

All answers are at the back of the book.

Quiz 41

You are looking for – a thing

1. I am an attraction
2. From 1925-1936 I advertised a car company with coloured bulbs visible from almost 20 miles away
3. There were protests about me and a petition was signed by 300 artists and intellectuals
4. Every 7 years I am painted
5. I am a building
6. I am 986 feet tall
7. There are more than 100 antennae on top of me for broadcasts
8. Charles Lindburgh used me as a beacon on his solo trans-Atlantic flight
9. I opened in 1889
10. It takes 60 tonnes of paint to cover me
11. I am in Paris
12. I was designed by Gustave Eiffel's company

The answer for this quiz is number 68.

All answers are at the back of the book.

Quiz 42

You are looking for – person or character

1. I died in Mayfair in London in 1910
2. My writings on religion and mysticism were only published after my death
3. I was part of a caring profession
4. I was a statistics pioneer
5. During my lifetime, my published writing was involved with spreading medical knowledge
6. I received the Royal Red Cross and the Order of Merit before I died
7. I was born on 12th May 1820 in Italy
8. I am female
9. My voice can be heard on an 1890 wax cylinder recording to raise money for veterans of the Charge of the Light Brigade
10. I was involved in the Crimean War
11. International Nurses Day is on my birthday
12. I was known as The Lady with the Lamp

The answer for this quiz is number 16.

All answers are at the back of the book.

Quiz 43

You are looking for – a year

1. The microwave oven is invented by Percy LeBaron Spence
2. Animal Farm by George Orwell is released
3. "A Hubba Hubba Hubba (Dig You Later)" by Perry Como is released
4. 1 ounce of gold cost $37.25
5. David Lloyd George, Prime Minister of the United Kingdom during the First World War, dies
6. *The Lost Weekend* directed by Billy Wilder came out this year and later won Best Film, Best Director and Best Actor at the Academy Awards
7. *Time* magazine's Man of the Year was Harry S. Truman
8. Actors Helen Mirren and Tom Seleck are born
9. The atomic bombings of Hiroshima and Nagasaki take place
10. The war in Europe ends, named VE Day
11. Adolf Hitler dies
12. The Second World War ends completely

The answer for this quiz is number 1.

All answers are at the back of the book.

Quiz 44

You are looking for – person or character

1. I am old
2. The name I am known by is not my real name
3. I am male
4. My job has a nice ring to it
5. I am not always the same person
6. I am expected to die in my job
7. I fell out with King Henry VIII
8. I have recently been Polish, German and Argentinian
9. I am the Bishop of Rome
10. My current name is Francis
11. I live in Vatican City
12. I am the head of the Catholic people of the world

The answer for this quiz is number 56.

All answers are at the back of the book.

Quiz 45

You are looking for – a thing

1. Individually I am small
2. I was used in the building of the Great Wall of China
3. I was first planted and grown in India, 4,000 years ago
4. I am part of the grass family
5. I am a food
6. The food poisoning bacteria bacillus cereus is a concern with me
7. I can be ground into flour
8. I am in some breakfast cereals
9. I can be egg fried, boiled or wild
10. I am mainly grown in Asia
11. I am a staple food for over half the world's population
12. Some of my varieties include long grain, short grain and arborio

The answer for this quiz is number 9.

All answers are at the back of the book.

Quiz 46

You are looking for – a place

1. In 2010, one of my 2,000 year old buildings collapsed prompting accusations of neglect
2. There is a lot of graffiti on me, and it is not from the modern day
3. I am a UNESCO World Heritage Site
4. Although I am a place, I am also a visitor attraction
5. My ruins were discovered in the 16th century, and I was excavated in the mid-18th century
6. Pliny the Younger provided an eye-witness account of a tragedy that happened to me
7. Emperor Nero visited me in around AD 64
8. AD 79 is an important date in my history
9. I am in Italy
10. I am at the base of Mount Vesuvius
11. Organic remains were used as moulds to make casts of people in their last moments alive here
12. In AD 79 the Mount Vesuvius erupted preserving my city under ash and volcanic debris

The answer for this quiz is number 30.

All answers are at the back of the book

Quiz 47

You are looking for – a thing

1. I can be collected
2. I can be used
3. Virtually all people in the world use me in some form
4. I am essential
5. I am used many billions of times every day
6. The first physical representation was made around 2,500 years ago
7. I am equivalent to a number
8. I can be plastic
9. Most of the time, my value goes down over time
10. It is considered lucky to find me unexpectedly
11. I can measure or store value
12. I am used to pay for things

The answer for this quiz is number 24.

All answers are at the back of the book.

Quiz 48

You are looking for – a person or character

1. I have three children
2. You might think I like animals
3. I am not keen on water
4. My father was called Lamech
5. I am a farmer
6. I am very old
7. I am best known for something I built
8. There are many films about me including one from 2007 with Steve Carell
9. I sent out a dove
10. I am in The Bible
11. I built an ark to avoid a flood
12. The animals came in two by two according to the song

The answer for this quiz is number 66.

All answers are at the back of the book.

Quiz 49

You are looking for – a thing

1. I am considered to be British
2. I like to serve
3. Historians believe I originated in France in the 12th century, but in a different form
4. I have a lot of love
5. Henry VIII enjoyed me
6. I am a game
7. I am descended from a game called jeu de paume
8. I am played on different surfaces
9. During a match, each player runs around 3 miles
10. I am played with a ball that used to be white
11. My balls can be served over 100mph
12. Serena and Venus Williams are famous sisters in my sport

The answer for this quiz is number 17.

All answers are at the back of the book.

Quiz 50

You are looking for – a person or character

1. I am an animal
2. I was originally conceived as a rabbit that could fight with my ears
3. My footwear design was taken from Michael Jackson's boots on the album sleeve for *Bad*
4. My style is similar to pop art
5. I am Japanese
6. I appear in places including South Island and Green Hill Zone
7. I am a cartoonish character
8. There have been at least two films and several TV series about me
9. I am best known for being in a computer game
10. I love gold rings
11. I am blue and spiky
12. I am a hedgehog

The answer for this quiz is number 48.

All answers are at the back of the book.

Quiz 51

You are looking for – a thing

1. I am used every day
2. Some parts of me are major household names
3. Most businesses want to use me
4. I am inside the majority of homes
5. I am extremely popular
6. I am part of a network
7. Crime related to me cost $3.5 billion for US businesses in 2019
8. I can be accessed in several different ways
9. Over 5 billion people use me worldwide
10. The dot com revolution was part of me
11. You can shop, learn and entertain yourself using me
12. I am on just about every computer and smartphone

The answer for this quiz is number 54.

All answers are at the back of the book.

Quiz 52

You are looking for – a year

1. Fire breaks out at The Winter Palace in St. Petersburg killing 30 guards
2. Mount Holyoke Female Seminary is founded to educate women in the USA
3. William Proctor and James Gamble begin selling in the USA – starting brand Proctor and Gamble
4. The daguerreotype is developed, the first publicly available photographic process
5. Wild Bill Hickok, western gunfighter, is born
6. Composer Chopin travels to London and plays at a musical soiree in James Broadwood's house
7. John Constable, painter of The Hay Wain dies
8. "God Save the Queen" is used for the first time as the national anthem in Great Britain
9. Samuel Morse files a patent for the telegraph
10. Martin Van Buren is sworn in as US President
11. Charles Dickens' *Oliver Twist* is first serialised
12. Queen Victoria comes to the throne at age 18 in Great Britain after her uncle dies

The answer for this quiz is number 73.

All answers are at the back of the book.

Quiz 53

You are looking for – a person or character

1. I am male
2. My clothes were originally described as being brown, tan or auburn red
3. I first appeared in a book called *The Little Bird* in 1902
4. I am in books and a play
5. My royalties were gifted to Great Ormond Street Hospital in 1929 and they still benefit from it today
6. "To die will be an awfully big adventure!" is a quote from my book
7. When I say play, it is often a pantomime these days
8. The first line of the book all about me, is "All children, except one, grow up"
9. My book was written by J.M. Barrie
10. My outfit these days is always green
11. Captain Hook is my rival
12. I live with the lost boys in Neverland

The answer for this quiz is number 3.

All answers are at the back of the book.

Quiz 54

You are looking for – a thing

1. I am reasonably common
2. Nobody wants me
3. There is a version of me named for Spain
4. I can make you feel hot
5. I am more likely to be around in the winter
6. My short name is only 3 letters long
7. I am passed around from person to person
8. I am constantly adapting
9. I can be deadly
10. I am a virus
11. You can be vaccinated against me each year
12. I am transmitted through sneezing, coughing and breathing via droplets

The answer for this quiz is number 26.

All answers are at the back of the book.

Quiz 55

You are looking for – a thing

1. I am a great insulator
2. I am solid
3. I can be measured
4. Children love me
5. I am made up of very small parts
6. I can be here today and gone tomorrow
7. An area in Japan is the place that typically has the most of me
8. I can cause closures
9. I am cold
10. I am a type of weather
11. I am something that is hoped for on Christmas Day
12. An igloo is made out of me

The answer for this quiz is number 67.

All answers are at the back of the book.

Quiz 56

You are looking for – a person or character

1. Various people have written about me, but one is best-known
2. I have a castle
3. I do not mind things being dirty
4. I appear in quite a few films – one in 1992 was directed by Francis Ford Coppola
5. I am not religious
6. My best-known author was the assistant of Sir Henry Irving and manager of the Lyceum Theatre
7. My name when translated from Romanian means "son of the dragon"
8. A real person also has my name and may have been my inspiration, he is Vlad the Impaler
9. I prefer to go out after dusk
10. My liquid diet is rather unusual
11. Bram Stoker wrote my story published in 1897
12. I am a vampire

The answer for this quiz is number 37.

All answers are at the back of the book

Quiz 57

You are looking for – a year

1. Vanatu, an island country in the South Pacific Ocean, gains independence
2. Evonne Goolagong Cawley wins the women's singles title at Wimbledon
3. The world's population is 4,434,682,000
4. The existence of Janus, a moon of Saturn is confirmed
5. The Talpiot Tomb is found in Jerusalem, thought at first to be the final resting place of Jesus
6. The song "Ashes to Ashes" by David Bowie is released
7. Robert Mugabe is elected as Prime Minister of Zimbabwe
8. Brazilian footballer Ronaldhino was born
9. The game Pac-Man is released in Japan
10. *The Twits* by Road Dahl is first published
11. The Rubik's cube makes its debut in London
12. John Lennon is assassinated in New York

The answer for this quiz is number 47.

All answers are at the back of the book.

Quiz 58

You are looking for – a person or character

1. I am dead
2. I took on great responsibility as a child
3. I am male
4. I had various illnesses including a cleft palette and a club foot
5. I was very rich
6. My homeland is steeped in history
7. I was a King
8. These days I am from Africa
9. I worshipped multiple gods
10. Not much would be known about me except for a discovery in 1922
11. Howard Carter is associated with me
12. My death mask is primarily gold with blue semi-precious stones

The answer for this quiz is number 18.

All answers are at the back of the book.

Quiz 59

You are looking for – a thing

1. I was invented by John Spilsbury in 1766
2. I come in a box
3. When I am whole, I am normally a standard shape
4. I can be very frustrating
5. I can be educational or just for fun
6. I am usually made from cardboard but used to be wooden
7. I am popular with all types of people, young and old
8. My pieces are all different shapes
9. Some people collect me
10. The largest of my kind is 551,232 pieces
11. My pieces tend to be in a multiple of 100 or 1000
12. If a piece is missing you cannot finish me

The answer for this quiz is number 55.

All answers are at the back of the book.

Quiz 60

You are looking for – a person or character

1. I was born in 1947
2. I own a radio station
3. I have been called a King
4. I have been in an unlikely band with other famous people from my profession
5. I collaborated with Michael Jackson in 1996 for the 40-minute music video *Ghosts*
6. I am American
7. When I was young, my childhood friend was hit and killed by a train
8. I am a writer
9. I am from Maine and many of my books are located here
10. My books have sold over 350 million copies
11. I am the King of Horror
12. I wrote *The Shining, It* and *Carrie*

The answer for this quiz is number 64.

All answers are at the back of the book.

Quiz 61

You are looking for - a place

1. You can find me in Britain
2. Former US President Bill Clinton proposed to his future wife Hillary here
3. I am northern
4. I am quite a wet place
5. I am home to a famous sausage
6. I am very popular, especially in summer
7. I contain the villages of Braithwaite, Caldbeck and Hawkshead
8. Arguably, the pencil was invented here
9. I contain a drowned village
10. A lot of hikers visit me
11. I contain England's highest mountain and deepest lake
12. I am a National Park

The answer for this quiz is number 10.

All answers are at the back of the book.

Quiz 62

You are looking for - a thing

1. I was invented in 1837 by Rowland Hill
2. Most countries have their own version of me
3. I am known not so much for what I am as what is done to me
4. I can be rare
5. I typically have a margin
6. I can be collected
7. The United Kingdom is the only country in the world not to print its name on me
8. New designs are made of me regularly
9. The first of me was released in 1840
10. I can be many different prices
11. My first types were black, blue and red
12. You need me to send a letter

The answer for this quiz is number 59.

All answers are at the back of the book.

Quiz 63

You are looking for – a person or character

1. I was born in 1570
2. I was a soldier in the Spanish army
3. I am quite a cheap guy
4. I came from a prominent Yorkshire family
5. I converted to Roman Catholicism
6. I was recruited in the Netherlands for a treasonous mission
7. I am a famous failure
8. I was a co-conspirator of Robert Catesby
9. I have a British political blog named after me
10. I was due to be hung, drawn and quartered but fell off the gallows and died instead
11. I am commemorated on a particular day each year in the UK
12. I took part in an explosive plot

The answer for this quiz is number 38.

All answers are at the back of the book.

Quiz 64

You are looking for - a thing

1. I can be very colourful
2. I can have a glass bottom
3. I appear to be extremely light
4. I was a result of brotherly ingenuity
5. Some might say I'm an old windbag
6. I am a form of transport
7. I can be an experience
8. 1783 was a first for me
9. I am quite slow
10. I have been used to monitor the weather
11. "Bud Light Spirit of Freedom" was the name of one of me
12. I am an early form of aviation

The answer for this quiz is number 46.

All answers are at the back of the book.

Quiz 65

You are looking for - a place

1. In a sense, I am out of time
2. When you are here, there's only one direction in which you can go
3. I am often dark
4. I float about
5. Many lines converge on me
6. It is disputed who found me first
7. There's a different scientific version of me
8. A needle points to me (sort of)
9. I'm witness to much shrinking
10. The nearest permanent habitation is over 500 miles from me
11. I have an opposite on the other side
12. Father Christmas lives here

The answer for this quiz is number 19.

All answers are at the back of the book.

Quiz 66

You are looking for – a person or character

1. I was an author and composer
2. I became a very senior religious figure
3. I was an accomplished athlete, huntsman and dancer
4. My nickname was Old Coppernose
5. I stole a lot of land and gave it to my friends
6. I married my brother's widow
7. I am known as the Father of the Royal Navy
8. I was born in a palace
9. I was very overweight in later life
10. I was a King
11. I had a daughter called Elizabeth and another called Mary
12. I was married six times

The answer for this quiz is number 28.

All answers are at the back of the book.

Quiz 67

You are looking for – a person or character

1. I am English
2. I was born in 1912
3. I received a PhD from Princeton University in 1938
4. I appear on a British banknote
5. A 2019 BBC TV Series named me the greatest person of the 20th century
6. Much of my work was covered by the Official Secrets Act
7. My 'children' may one day explore the universe
8. I was prosecuted for being gay
9. I was a mathematician
10. I came up with a famous test, which has never yet been passed
11. I was instrumental in cracking the Enigma Code
12. I worked at Bletchley Park during World War 2

The answer for this quiz is number 36.

All answers are at the back of the book.

Quiz 68

You are looking for - a thing

1. I am very small
2. I am thin
3. I am clear
4. My invention is credited to either Louis J Girard or Adolf Fick, but Leonardo da Vinci had an early concept of me
5. I am usually invisible
6. Many people use different ones of me every day
7. I am made with different types of plastic
8. Most people don't sleep with me
9. I am worn
10. Over two thirds of my wearers are women
11. I help people see
12. I can be used instead of glasses

The answer for this quiz is number 11.

All answers are at the back of the book.

Quiz 69

You are looking for – a place

1. I am on the coast
2. I am an anagram of my predecessor
3. I have a Skytree
4. I am a city
5. I have the most Michelin starred restaurants of any city in the world
6. I was originally due to host the Olympic Games in 1940, but that did not happen and eventually I hosted it in 1964
7. I used to be called Edo
8. I am in Asia
9. By one definition, I'm the most populated city on Earth
10. I have thousands of temples
11. I have many capsule hotels
12. I am the capital of Japan

The answer for this quiz is number 71.

All answers are at the back of the book.

Quiz 70

You are looking for - a thing

1. My earliest ancestor dates back to the Levant in the 2nd millennium B.C.
2. I used to include thorn
3. I can have many different shapes
4. My most recent loss was a frequently used symbol
5. I can be upper or lower
6. My upper is often straighter
7. Sweden and Portugal use me, but Russia does not
8. Officially I'm Roman or Latin
9. I am named after two Greek letters
10. I make words
11. There are 26 parts of me
12. On a computer keyboard I'm all mixed up

The answer for this quiz is number 40.

All answers are at the back of the book.

Quiz 71

You are looking for – a person or character

1. I was born in 1879
2. I became an American in 1940
3. As a child I was profoundly inspired by two things: a compass and a geometry book
4. I have a very recognisable face
5. I wrote many papers
6. I called nationalism the "measles of mankind"
7. I was born in Ulm, Germany
8. I became deeply religious at the age of 12
9. I won the Nobel Prize
10. I am known for both special and general reasons
11. My hair is rather wild
12. I'm best known for my theories of relativity

The answer for this quiz is number 62.

All answers are at the back of the book.

Quiz 72

You are looking for – a place

1. There are many places in the world named after me
2. According to the UN definition, I can be classified as a forest
3. My name is thought to be Roman in origin
4. I have many parks
5. A river runs through me
6. I allegedly have more Indian restaurants than Mumbai
7. I am officially the smallest city in the UK
8. My underground railway network was the first in the world (and originally steam powered!)
9. I have hosted the Olympic Games 3 times
10. I have a population of around 9 million
11. I had a Great Fire in 1666
12. I am home to Buckingham Palace

The answer for this quiz is number 21.

All answers are at the back of the book.

Quiz 73

You are looking for – a thing

1. People live in me
2. I am around the size of a five bedroomed house inside
3. I am used to discover more about being in a unique environment
4. I am involved in experiments of different kinds
5. Susan Helms was the first woman to visit me, in 2001
6. Part of me is called Tranquility
7. People from over 18 countries have visited me
8. You have to know some Russian to come to me
9. I was launched in 1998
10. Chris Hadfield, Sergei Krikalev and Tim Peake are some of the best-known names associated with me
11. I orbit the Earth 16 times every 24 hours
12. Only astronauts can stay here

The answer for this quiz is number 58.

All answers are at the back of the book.

Quiz 74

You are looking for – a person or character

1. I was a preacher in England for a time
2. I am a painter
3. I had difficulties with mental health and spent a year in an asylum
4. I painted The Potato Eaters
5. I had a studio in Arles, France and created many paintings of this area
6. I am Dutch
7. I committed suicide
8. I painted over 900 paintings but only sold one during my lifetime
9. One of my most famous paintings is The Starry Night
10. Part of my ear was cut off
11. In 1990, one of my paintings sold for $75m
12. My initials are VVG

The answer for this quiz is number 7.

All answers are at the back of the book.

Quiz 75

You are looking for – a thing

1. I was inspired by a trip to the beach
2. I was separately invented by Joseph Woodland and George Laurer
3. A version of me was first used on railway cars
4. Wrigley's Gum was a first for me
5. I was originally shaped like a bullseye
6. I helped big businesses get bigger
7. Some people get a tattoo of me, usually as a protest
8. I am black and white
9. A UPC is an integral part of me
10. I am usually read by a laser
11. I usually have 12 or 13 digits
12. Most things you buy have me

The answer for this quiz is number 43.

All answers are at the back of the book.

Answers Section

Answer Number 1 (for Quiz Number 43)

Answer – 1945. On VE day, Princesses Elizabeth and Margaret (Elizabeth of course became Queen Elizabeth II of the United Kingdom) were allowed to go out to join the celebrations. Princess Elizabeth wore her Auxiliary Transport Service uniform and said in 1985 that she was concerned about being recognised by members of the public so pulled her uniform cap down over her eyes!

Answer Number 2 (for Quiz Number 6)

Answer – The Equator. The equator is effectively a line drawn around the centre of the Earth. It is marked in certain countries like Brazil by a physical landmark. To the top and bottom of the earth are the Arctic and Antarctic and in the middle between each of these and the equator, are the Tropic of Cancer and the Tropic of Capricorn. These five 'lines' on the earth are linked.

Answer Number 3 (for Quiz Number 53)

Answer - Peter Pan. He first appeared as a character in J.M. Barrie's book *The Little Bird* but gained his own book a few years later and that is how we best know him. Disney popularised his outfit to green and now, if he was given a different colour no one would know who he was.

Answer Number 4 (for Quiz Number 12)

Answer – Goldilocks. The basis of the Goldilocks fairy story was by Robert Southey in 1837. There are three iterations of the story, the first being about an unpleasant elderly woman going into the house of three bachelor bears while they are away. The story we know these days is a rather less unpleasant version and involves Goldilocks eating the porridge belonging to the family of three bears and sleeping in their beds!

Answer Number 5 (for Quiz Number 20)

Answer – Mediterranean Sea. The beautiful jewel in the crown of Europe. There are an impressive 190 islands and over 24 countries along the Mediterranean Sea and not all European. It is almost completely contained by land hence being almost landlocked.

Answer Number 6 (for Quiz Number 28)

Answer – *Jurassic Park*. The idea of cloning dinosaurs from their preserved DNA, while science fiction, is not beyond the realms of belief. Children and adults alike are fascinated by the idea of dinosaurs and this film has everything – a great concept, acting, directing and soundtrack. It also had a generous budget allowing for excellent effects.

Answer Number 7 (for Quiz Number 74)

Answer: Vincent Van Gogh. His achievements are all the more impressive when you realise that most of the 900 or so paintings he created were done in the last 2 years of his life. One of the most famous stories about Van Gogh is that he cut off his ear. How much of that is true is unknown. Part of this ear was cut off following an argument with fellow artist Paul Gaugin, but one theory suggests it was Gaugin who cut off Van Gogh's ear with a sword during the altercation. Van Gogh then gave his ear to a girl who was a maid at a brothel; she promptly fainted on the spot – or so the story goes.

Answer Number 8 (for Quiz Number 36)

Answer – Cuba. A beautiful island full of history with its gorgeous colourful buildings in Havana. You can see plenty of American classic cars on the roads, lovingly cared for by their owners. Tobacco is a huge export and Cuban cigars are thought to be the very best in the world. They are still banned in the USA as are all exports due to a trade embargo from 1962 that still exists. It is actually not illegal to smoke a Cuban cigar, it is just illegal to buy or sell them!

Answer Number 9 (for Quiz Number 45)

Answer – Rice. A staple food that is a large constituent of the meals of many people around the world. Roughly 90% of the world's rice is grown in Asia and it is a principal food across many Asian countries. Rice is enclosed by a husk. When this is removed but the bran is left behind, it is brown rice. When the bran is also removed that makes white rice but taking the bran away removes most of the good nutrients as well.

Answer Number 10 (for Quiz Number 61)

Answer – The Lake District (or Cumbria). The village of Mardale Green was once one of the most beautiful villages in the Lake District and home to hundreds of residents, however it was abandoned in 1935. The church and village pub closed, and the residents of the village were evicted so that the valley it was in could be flooded to construct a reservoir to supply the nearby city of Manchester with drinking water. The reservoir, Haweswater, is four miles long and half a mile wide. During particularly dry summers, the water level drops significantly, and the ruins of the village can be seen.

Answer Number 11 (for Quiz Number 68)

Answer: Contact Lens. Early designs of contact lenses can't have been much fun to wear, and often were impractical. None more so than Leonardo da Vinci's design, which involved dunking your face (and hence the eyes) in a clear bowl of water!

Answer Number 12 (for Quiz Number 1)

Answer – Fire. The ability to cook food, is often described as what sets humans apart from animals. It is an essential component of everyday life although not in the format of an open fire for heating and cooking – unless you really love barbecues. From wildfires to candle flames, there are many types of fire, and we should not underestimate its ability to be destructive.

Answer Number 13 (for Quiz Number 14)

Answer – Madagascar. A place world renowned for unique and biologically interesting flora and fauna, most of which is found nowhere else on Earth. Sadly, some species are in decline as humankind destroys its natural habitat. Cocoa is a product helping to give some of the island inhabitants produce to sell. Grown on small farms, it is delicious yet rare and can fetch a high price.

Answer Number 14 (for Quiz Number 23)

Answer – Amazon. Love it or hate it, Amazon is a global brand that most people know. It features an easy ordering system and the opportunity to buy it today and have it to your door tomorrow. It also has a range of 'own brand' products from Amazon Prime TV, Echo devices with Alexa and tablets/ e-readers with the Kindle Fire and Amazon Kindle. It employed 1,289,000 people worldwide in 2020.

Answer Number 15 (for Quiz Number 31)

Answer – 1620. A pretty tricky year to find, but they cannot all be easy! Hopefully some of the clues allowed you to narrow it down somewhat. Peregrine White was the first known English child born to Pilgrims in America as he arrived when the Mayflower was docked in what is now Cape Cod.

Answer Number 16 (for Quiz Number 42)

Answer – Florence Nightingale. She established a nursing school at St Thomas' Hospital in London and International Nurses Day is still celebrated on her birthday. She was also a statistician and created the polar area diagram pie chart. She was a prolific writer on many different topics. She was educated by her father, receiving a socially advanced education for a woman which likely affected her life decisions.

Answer Number 17 (for Quiz Number 49)

Answer – Tennis. A popular sport these days, but did you know it was a favourite of King Henry VIII of England too? It is descended from a French game called jeu de paume, where the palm of the hand was used instead of a racquet. From clay to grass, it is possible to play on a multitude of surfaces.

Answer Number 18 (for Quiz Number 58)

Answer – Tutankhamun. The boy King of Egypt who died young. We only really know about Tutankhamun as when his tomb was found in 1922 by Howard Carter, it had not been significantly looted like almost all other tombs. This tomb has given us a huge amount of insight into the life and death of ancient Egyptians. Many of the priceless artefacts are kept at the Egyptian Museum in Cairo.

Answer Number 19 (for Quiz Number 65)

Answer - North Pole. Unlike the South Pole, the North Pole is not actually land because there isn't any up there! The

Geographic North Pole is actually on a sheet of ice, which shifts about each year. If you manage to get there, there is only one direction you can go, which is south. You are already north here and there is no east or west because you are literally at the top of the world! Confusingly if you follow a compass, it won't actually take you there, it will take you to the Magnetic North Pole, which is in Canada. The reason they are different is... complicated!

Answer Number 20 (for Quiz Number 8)

Answer – A bubble. It is a simple thing – it aerates drinks or is the result of a soapy bowl of water or a bath. It is in fact a complicated and clever scientific process.

Answer Number 21 (for Quiz Number 72)

Answer – London. In these quizzes it is always fun to find clues that send you, the reader, in the wrong direction. There are two particular clues here that do this. Firstly, London is technically a forest because of its many parks. The UN definition is of "land spanning more than 0.5 hectares with trees higher than 5 meters and a canopy cover of more than 10%". The other mis-directing clue is that London is officially the smallest city in the UK. This is because it is technically the "City of London", which is the small financial district of the wider city.

Answer Number 22 (for Quiz Number 16)

Answer – Elon Musk. He is consistently one of the richest people in the world but typically describes himself as cash poor. He is an interesting character having come from a very wealthy family. He got into internet businesses at a good time and has built up his wealth through clever developments and canny investments. A huge amount of controversy follows him around, from his connection to Jeffrey Epstein to complaints about his managerial style.

Answer Number 23 (for Quiz Number 32)

Answer - James Bond. The first James Bond novel by Ian Fleming appeared in 1953. That was *Casino Royale*, and the film *Dr No* followed 10 years later in 1963. They are still being created today with controversy always following the question of who "will be the next Bond?" He has his villains and his glamorous Bond Girls like Pussy Galore, although they are being toned down somewhat for a modern audience!

Answer Number 24 (for Quiz Number 47)

Answer – Money. The idea of bartering was around over 10,000 years ago, so I give you some wheat and you give me some meat. Exchanging goods for money is a much later invention, so from around 2,500 years ago when the first coins were made. Paper money came from China only around 1,000 years ago. The most traded currency in the world is the United States Dollar.

Answer Number 25 (for Quiz Number 24)

Answer – Titanic. It is simply the most infamous cruise ship disaster in history. The lack of lifeboats was an important factor. The 20 lifeboats could carry only around half of the passengers on board and the first lifeboats were not full. This inevitably led to passengers not able to get a lifeboat and being in the sea. The water was around 28 °F or -2 °C potentially leading to hypothermia within 15 minutes. Few people survived from the water as it took hours to be rescued, although head baker Charles Joughin ended up treading water for 2 hours before being rescued by a lifeboat. He was drunk and this might have kept him calmer, allowing him to avoid cold shock response!

Answer Number 26 (for Quiz Number 54)

Answer – Influenza. Influenza or flu as it is better known is still a deadly disease. People often mistake a bad cold for flu, but if you have had it, you will know how rotten it makes you feel. If you get influenza remember fluids, rest and painkillers and most people get better on their own, in time.

Answer Number 27 (for Quiz Number 4)

Answer - The Year 2000. The new millennium (although some might argue that's 2001), lots of memorable things happened in this year. From engaging movies to world events this is a year many of us will have in living memory. Do you remember the millennium bug and the impact people thought it might have on computers around the world?

Answer Number 28 (for Quiz Number 66)

Answer: Henry VIII. He has something of a reputation these days – mainly for having so many wives but also for being overweight and unhealthy. However, it wasn't always so, and earlier on in his life he was an accomplished athlete and hunter. He was also a very successful monarch, who laid the groundwork for the golden age of the Elizabethan Era under his daughter Elizabeth I. If he hadn't massively expanded the Royal Navy, the English would never have been able to defeat the Spanish Armada, and the history of the world might have been very different.

Answer Number 29 (for Quiz Number 38)

Answer - John F Kennedy. Known as JFK, he is probably better known now for his death than his life. On 22nd November 1963, he was assassinated in Dallas. Lee Harvey Oswald was arrested just 70 minutes after the shooting by which time JFK had already died. Oswald was killed two days later while in police custody by a local nightclub owner, Jack Ruby.

Answer Number 30 (for Quiz Number 46)

Answer – Pompeii.A fascinating snapshot of a historic past, the volcanic eruption lasted two days and some people were trapped under the ash, which left their outline behind. These were filled with plaster and the moulds of the people were removed. These are one of the highlights of Pompeii as an attraction. It is under state control but calls to be privatised came in 2010 after a 2,000 year old "House of Gladiators" fell down after inadequate protection.

Answer Number 31 (for Quiz Number 17)

Answer – The Olympics. Although the Olympics had been an ancient Greek phenomenon, the modern Olympics began in 1896. From the Olympic flame (the hot bit!) to the five rings, it is a measure of sporting success in many countries.

Countries who host the Olympics often find financing it a huge burden, although it does bring together people from most countries of the world. Even North Korea generally takes part, although not in Tokyo 2020 due to concerns over Covid.

Answer Number 32 (for Quiz Number 10)

Answer – 1901. A big year in both the UK and USA as events rocked these nations. However, it was also a time of change and development that would begin to shape the new century for the whole world.

Answer Number 33 (for Quiz Number 26)

Answer – Monopoly. The most recognisable board game in the world. It has been licensed in over 103 countries and printed in over 37 languages. The original tokens were battleship, top hat, race car, boot, thimble, iron, cannon, lantern, purse and rocking horse. Lantern, purse and rocking horse were retired within 5 years and were replaced with dog, wheelbarrow, horse and rider. In 1998, a money bag was added to make 11 pieces. The cannon and horse rider were retired in 2000 and the money bag was then retired in 2007. In 2013 a Facebook poll had the cat replace the iron. In 2017, the thimble, wheelbarrow and boot were retired. They were replaced with a penguin, Tyrannosaurus Rex and a rubber duck.

Answer Number 34 (for Quiz Number 40)

Answer – Steven Spielberg. He is the world's most commercially successful director and has won plenty of accolades. He co-founded Amblin Entertainment and Dreamworks and has produced many films as well as directed. Mostly Spielberg films have a soundtrack composed by John Williams – in fact there are only five feature films where the music was composed by someone else.

Answer Number 35 (for Quiz Number 33)

Answer – Snake. A "love them or hate them" kind of animal. Snakes were mentioned in the Bible, notably in the Garden of Eden, hence their bad reputation going back many years. The most venomous snakes are the Saw-Scaled Viper and King Cobra which attack with a bite that contains venom. There are also constrictors like anacondas which wrap around and then squeeze until death.

Answer Number 36 (for Quiz Number 67)

Answer: Alan Turing. He played an important role in defeating Hitler in World War II through his work with codebreakers at Bletchley Park. He also laid the foundations of the technological revolution due to his work on computers and Artificial Intelligence. He gives his name to the Turing Test, a test to determine if Artificial Intelligence can fool human observers into thinking it is human – it has never yet been passed by any machine.

Answer Number 37 (for Quiz Number 56)

Answer – Dracula. Count Dracula is a story written by Irish author Bram Stoker and from his Transylvanian castle he travels to England in boxes of dirt from his homeland to plague Whitby. Stoker researched Dracula while on holiday in Whitby and his inspiration may have been Vlad the Impaler, also called Vlad Dracula. Dracula only comes out at night and feasts on human blood. In many film adaptations, Dracula is a kind of devil and can therefore be hurt or burned by the sign of the cross.

Answer Number 38 (for Quiz Number 63)

Answer: Guy Fawkes. It does seem unfair that Guy Fawkes is such a pantomime villain in Britain, when he was just the hired help rather than the instigator of the gunpowder plot. However almost all the co-conspirators were executed so they got their come-uppance! The plan was to blow up the Houses of Parliament on the occasion of the State Opening, and today the cellars are searched by the Yeoman of the Guard before the State Opening of Parliament each year, although this is now mostly just a quaint custom in addition to the more rigorous anti-terrorism precautions that regularly take place!

Answer Number 39 (for Quiz Number 5)

Answer – Buddha. He was a real person – probably a step away from the grinning Buddha we see these days! Immortalised in everything from solid gold to candle wax with a wick protruding from the top of his head, he is a symbol of joy. Buddhism is a very important worldwide religion, especially in Asia. Over 500 million people worldwide are Buddhist which is 7% or 8% of the world's population.

Answer Number 40 (for Quiz Number 70)

Answer – The Alphabet. The English alphabet hasn't always been 26 letters long. As late as the 19th century, school children in America were taught that there were 27 letters, the 27th and final letter of the alphabet being the ampersand

"&" symbol. Before that, there were various different letters including Thorn, Wynn and Ash. You still see glimpses of some of these letters today. Thorn looked like 'Y' in gothic style scripting, and so the letter Y was used in its stead on continental printing presses which didn't have the letter Thorn. It was gradually being replaced with 'th' anyway, but still clings on in old signs that say 'Ye olde…'

Answer Number 41 (for Quiz Number 13)

Answer – *Frozen*. The *Frozen* film was inspired by Hans Christian Andersen's fairy tale *The Snow Queen* although took quite a departure from this in the end. It was highly praised and was considered to be the studios' best animated film since its renaissance era. It became the highest grossing film of 2013, receiving two Academy Awards.

Answer Number 42 (for Quiz Number 21)

Answer – Gold. It is a very soft metal with the atomic number 79 and the chemical symbol Au. Around 50% of all gold is made into jewellery and it is used for wedding rings. Pure gold is 24 carats, but this is not suitable as jewellery as it is far too soft, so it needs to be mixed with another metal to reduce the carats and make it more useable.

Answer Number 43 (for Quiz Number 75)

Answer: A barcode. This came about out of a need to easily categorise and label different products quickly. The story of its invention is an interesting one, but the larger story is the commercial and social change which its invention made possible. The rise of big retail conglomerates would certainly have been much slower without the humble barcode.

Answer Number 44 (for Quiz Number 29)

Answer - Frida Kahlo. She has become extremely popular in recent times. Her story has inspired people as she persevered despite pain and suffering and was not a traditional beauty but was a strong-minded and successful woman. Her art is similarly bold and inspires current trends and prints.

Answer Number 45 (for Quiz Number 39)

Answer – Amazon River. The Amazon River is the largest river by discharge volume of water in the world although length is all about how you measure it, and the Nile is longer these days. It was first explored scientifically by Charles Marie de la Condamine in 1743.

Answer Number 46 (for Quiz Number 64)

Answer: Hot Air Balloon. The Hot Air Balloon was invented by the Mongolfier brothers, more than a century before the more famous Wright brothers launched a powered aircraft flight. The Mongolfier Brothers were the first to achieve a manned balloon flight, in a balloon made partly of paper (their day job was that of paper manufacturers). Two months earlier, they'd launched an unmanned balloon in front of Louis XVI and the royal family. It's cargo? A sheep, a duck and a cockerel. It soared to 600 metres in the air before getting a puncture and slowly sinking back to earth. The animals were all fine; they were hailed as "heroes of the air" and lived out their days in the Menagerie in Versailles.

Answer Number 47 (for Quiz Number 57)

Answer – 1980. A year with plenty going on, it was a time of fragile peace and trouble brewing. On the other hand, there were plenty of great songs and books to choose from that are in the living memory of many people.

Answer Number 48 (for Quiz Number 50)

Answer - Sonic the Hedgehog. He is an iconic cartoon figure with his blue spikes. The ringing of Sonic collecting a gold ring is a well-known sound to most gamers. Its popularity since the game's release in 1991 has led to several recent films, taking it in a new direction.

Answer Number 49 (for Quiz Number 35)

Answer – Mary Poppins. P.L.Travers based Mary Poppins on her early life in Australia although she lived most of her own life in England. Mary Poppins comes to right unruly families and goes when the wind changes, whether you want her to or not. The 1964 film with Julie Andrews is an interesting take on the books although P.L. Travers herself was not particularly happy with it. It took Walt Disney 20 years to keep his promise to his children and to get her to give him the rights to make the film.

Answer Number 50 (for Quiz Number 2)

Answer – Amsterdam. Amsterdam is a capital city and holds a huge amount of charm. It is a place where you can while away an hour in a coffee house or a local microbrewery, or enjoy an invigorating boat trip on one of the canals. It is a liberal place where some vices are legalised. From historical sights to more modern offerings, it makes a great location for tourists.

Answer Number 51 (for Quiz Number 19)

Answer – Queen Elizabeth II. When her uncle abdicated in 1936, after one year in office, her life changed forever. Her father was only 56 when he died leaving her at 25 to become Queen of the United Kingdom, Head of the Commonwealth and queen regnant of seven independent Commonwealth countries. She has enjoyed many jubilees and became the longest reigning monarch of the UK in 2015 surpassing her great-great grandmother Queen Victoria. On 27th May 2024 she will become the longest-reigning monarch of a sovereign state, surpassing Louis XIV of France.

Answer Number 52 (for Quiz Number 27)

Answer – Las Vegas. A world-renowned resort city, it is well-known as a place for shopping, entertainment and fine dining as well as nightlife and gambling. Notable features are the "Strip", popular helicopter rides and the hotels. There's the Bellagio's dancing fountains, The Mirage with an erupting volcano and the Venetian hotel with its gondola rides as well as a Paris hotel with a replica Eiffel Tower!

Answer Number 53 (for Quiz Number 11)

Answer- Africa. This is perhaps a bit of a trick question because you may have been expecting a country or a city. Africa is the second biggest continent by both area and population, after Asia. It is generally considered the 'Cradle of Civilisation', as the scientific consensus is that everyone is descended from Homo Sapiens who left Africa 60,000 years ago.

Answer Number 54 (for Quiz Number 51)

Answer – The Internet. A few internet facts:

- There are almost two billion websites online
- Over 7 million blog posts get published every day
- Over 500 hours of video are uploaded to YouTube every minute
- Over 4 billion of the people who use the internet access it on a phone

Answer Number 55 (for Quiz Number 59)

Answer – Jigsaw. As we know them now, jigsaws were created by mapmaker John Spilsbury in the 1760s by cutting up a map as an educational toy for children. What a wonderful invention that has given so much pleasure to people for many years.

Answer Number 56 (for Quiz Number 44)

Answer – The Pope. In his white cassock, he is a well-known figure across the world. To decide a pope, a papal conclave of the College of Cardinals gets together in the Sistine Chapel in Vatican City. They need to decide who will be Pope. The person who is chosen is given the choice whether to accept, and since the year 533, the new Pope is also free to choose his regnal name.

Answer Number 57 (for Quiz Number 37)

Answer – Rose. A beautiful flower that can adorn gardens outdoors and be cut for decoration indoors. They have a wonderful scent that is well-known. There are many varieties and types of roses from tea rose to dog rose and damask rose, which all have their own unique scent.

Answer Number 58 (for Quiz Number 73)

Answer - International Space Station. The ISS is a beacon and travels at 17,500 mph at an altitude of 250 miles. NASA is using it to discover more about living and working in space. Parts of the ISS were made in Russia and are operated by Roscosmos. They manage all of the guidance, navigation and control for the entire station. This is why the whole crew must be able to speak Russian and English.

Answer Number 59 (for Quiz Number 62)

Answer: Postage Stamp. The Penny Black was the world's first postage stamp, coming out in 1840 with the image of the new Queen Victoria on it. Since then, the UK's stamps have all had the reigning monarch's head as evidence of origin, rather than the name of the country. More than 68 million Penny Black stamps were printed, so they aren't that expensive for collectors, although you are looking at a four-figure sum for a mint condition one.

Answer Number 60 (for Quiz Number 22)

Answer - Greta Thunberg. Born in 2003, it was only in 2018 that Greta began spending Fridays outside Swedish Parliament calling for action on climate change. She is known for challenging world leaders to take action. She has received many honours and awards and continues as an ambassador against climate change.

Answer Number 61 (for Quiz Number 30)

Answer - Taj Mahal. The Taj Mahal is one of the most iconic buildings in the world. If we had given you a picture, you would probably have known it on sight and not needed any clues! It was built over a period of 22 years after being commissioned in 1632 by Mughal emperor Shah Jahan for the tomb of his favourite wife Mumtaz Mahal. It was designated a UNESCO World Heritage site in 1983.

Answer Number 62 (for Quiz Number 71)

Answer - Albert Einstein. There's not a lot else to say about Einstein – he's one of the most famous people of the 20th century, his hair even more so. It may surprise you to discover he was deeply religious, but it didn't last long – he abandoned religion in favour of science when he was a teenager. While he fell out with religion, it is generally thought he believed in an impersonal creator.

Answer Number 63 (for Quiz Number 7)

Answer – Electricity. It was discovered some time ago although natural lightning was seen before this time. Some in the Roman times thought that lightning was a sign from God that he was unhappy with man. There is much speculation that the Egyptians might have used electricity. This is mainly due to misinformation regarding copper topped poles and a lack of soot from naked flames in the tomb of Tutankhamun. We never said this speculation was correct!

Answer Number 64 (for Quiz Number 60)

Answer - Stephen King. So much to say, but did you know that the band is called The Rock Bottom Remainders and features authors including Mitch Albom, Amy Tan and Matt Groening of *The Simpsons* fame! He has published 63 novels, 5 non-fiction books and 200 or so short stories. That is certainly prolific!

Answer Number 65 (for Quiz Number 15)

Answer – Clock. An instrument that measures time. Early versions were made with water and sundials are still easy to make today. Everyone wants a clock to give them more time, whether that's hours in the day or more time at the end of life.

Answer Number 66 (for Quiz Number 48)

Answer – Noah. Biblical character Noah makes a wooden ark to protect himself and his family as well as two of each animal to save them from a flood sent by God. Impressive, considering he was meant to be over 500 years old at the time!

Answer Number 67 (for Quiz Number 55)

Answer – Snow. Thanks to the air pockets within snow, it is a great insulator. That is why it makes an igloo warm when the only actual warmth comes from your own body heat. A white Christmas is an important part of folklore, and this is something that in the UK, people can bet on. The amount of snowfall you need to determine a White Christmas is simply one single flake!

Answer Number 68 (for Quiz Number 41)

Answer - Eiffel Tower. The Eiffel Tower is the very chic of Paris in France. It was only meant to last 20 years and then be taken down for scrap, but it still stands as proud as ever. A trip to the top is a must when visiting the city.

Answer Number 69 (for Quiz Number 34)

Answer – Birthday Card. The oldest known birthday message was written on a wooden tablet from a Roman woman, dug up at Vindolanda Roman Fort in Hexham, UK. Thankfully in later times a more practical way to wish someone happy birthday was found in the birthday card. In a recent survey by Hallmark, they found that most cards are bought by women, by a large margin. Also, birthday cards are the most popular of their kind – they are the most purchased single card, above anniversaries and Valentine's Day.

Answer Number 70 (for Quiz Number 25)

Answer – Samuel L Jackson. He has a huge number of impressive films under his belt as an actor. From *Shaft* to *The Hateful Eight*, to his major roles with Star Wars and the Marvel franchises, he is in great demand. In 1968 at the age of 19, Jackson attended the funeral of Martin Luther King Jr as an usher. He was involved with the Black Power movement at one point, having attended segregated schools in Tennessee as a child.

Answer Number 71 (for Quiz Number 69)

Answer: Tokyo. Word geeks will be fascinated to discover that Kyoto was the previous capital of Tokyo, and Kyoto and Tokyo are anagrams of each other. They sound similar, because in Japanese Kyoto means "imperial capital" and Tokyo means "imperial capital east".

Answer Number 72 (for Quiz Number 3)

Answer – Harry Potter. The boy wizard makes a captivating set of seven books written by J K Rowling. These are the best-selling novel series ever, with over 500 million copies sold. Harry finds one day that he is a wizard and attends

Hogwarts School of Witchcraft and Wizardry, meeting his friends Ron and Hermione. Together they work to fight an evil overlord who threatens the fabric of wizard society once again. Oh, and his red house is his school house, Gryffindor!

Answer Number 73 (for Quiz Number 52)

Answer – 1837. An interesting year by all accounts, with plenty of events happening all over the world, some good and some, like wars, not so positive.

Answer Number 74 (for Quiz Number 18)

Answer – Jupiter. The fifth planet from the Sun, the biggest in the solar system and the third brightest natural item in the sky. Jupiter is increasingly being investigated by probes. The Juno probe left Earth on 5th August 2011 and arrived in Jupiter's orbit on 4th July 2016. Missions to Jupiter are long-term investments and high cost – this was $1.1 billion but is expected to yield fascinating results when it finally returns to Earth.

Answer Number 75 (for Quiz Number 9)

Answer – Sherlock Holmes. He first appeared in *A Study in Scarlet*, the first of four novels as well as fifty-six short stories and there is plenty to enjoy for any fan of the fictional detective. From Inspector Lestrade to Moriarty, there are some great accompanying parts that make the stories so good. Step back in time at the 221B Baker Street Museum in London for an interesting look at this most famous of addresses!

Printed in Great Britain
by Amazon

77969421R00068